Costume Through the Ages

Over 1400 Illustrations

ERHARD KLEPPER

DOVER PUBLICATIONS, INC.
Mineola, New York

PUBLISHER'S NOTE

Costume Through the Ages consists of 1225 numbered illustrations (counting the unnumbered ones, there are over 1440 altogether) drawn and arranged by Erhard Klepper. In an unbroken series of drawings, this volume represents 1900 years of costume—from the 1st century until 1930. What helps lend the book its unique character as an unusually valuable reference tool is the almost total lack of interpretation brought to bear upon subject matter that might otherwise—in a slightly less scholarly spirit—be infused with the idiom of the day.

Culled from a myriad of sources ancient and modern—including statuary, sculpture, mosaics, monuments, illuminated manuscripts, paintings, engravings, caricatures, lithographs, fashion plates, photographs, and magazines—the work achieves its avowed aim of preserving the essential lines of the clothing depicted, while meticulously rendering each and every precious detail. The numbers that accompany most of the illustrations correspond to "Notes on the Sources" at the end of the book.

Bibliographical Note

This Dover edition, first published in 1999, is an unabridged republication of the work originally published in 1961 by F. A. Herbig, Germany, under the title *Das Büchlein der tausend Kostüme.*

Library of Congress Cataloging-in-Publication Data

Klepper, Erhard.
    [Büchlein der tausend Kostüme. English]
    Costume through the ages : over 1400 illustrations / Erhard Klepper.
        p.   cm.
    Includes bibliographical references.
    ISBN 0-486-40722-5 (pbk.)
    1. Costume—Pictorial works. I. Title.
GT513.K513   1999
391—dc21
                                            99-37497
                                             CIP

Manufactured in the United States of America
Dover Publications, Inc., 31 East 2nd Street, Mineola, N.Y. 11501

FIRST CENTURY

1

FIRST AND SECOND CENTURIES

FOURTH AND FIFTH CENTURIES

NINTH TO ELEVENTH CENTURIES

1

2

3

4

5

6

7

TWELFTH CENTURY

THIRTEENTH CENTURY

1   2   3   4   5   6

THIRTEENTH CENTURY

1

2

3

4

5

THIRTEENTH CENTURY

FOURTEENTH CENTURY

1

2

3

4

5

FOURTEENTH CENTURY

FOURTEENTH CENTURY

1

2

3

4

5

6

7

FIFTEENTH CENTURY

FIFTEENTH CENTURY

FIFTEENTH CENTURY

FIFTEENTH CENTURY

SIXTEENTH CENTURY

SIXTEENTH CENTURY

SIXTEENTH CENTURY

SIXTEENTH CENTURY

SIXTEENTH CENTURY

SIXTEENTH CENTURY

SIXTEENTH CENTURY

SIXTEENTH CENTURY

1

2

3

4

5

6

7

8

9

10

11

12

13

SEVENTEENTH CENTURY

SEVENTEENTH CENTURY

SEVENTEENTH CENTURY

SEVENTEENTH CENTURY

SEVENTEENTH CENTURY

SEVENTEENTH CENTURY

1

2

3

4

5

1721–30

1741-50

1751–60

1   2   3   4

5   6   7   8

1771-80

1781–90

1793-94

1   2

3

4

5

6   7

1795-96

1795–96

1799–1800

1   2   3   4

5   6   7

8   9   10   11   12

1800–1803

1804-1807

1   2   3   4   5

6   7

8   9   10   11   12   13

1   2   3

4

5   6   7   8   9   10

11   12   13   14   15   16

1818-21

1   2   3   4   5
6   7   8   9
10   11   12   13   14   15

1822-24

1825-27

1831–32

1833-34

1835–37

1838–40

1841–44

1848–50

1 2 3 4 5 6

7 8

9 9

9

10 11 12 13

9

14 15 16 17 18 19

1853-54

1858–60

1861-62

1863–64

1865–67

1868–70

1 2 3 4 5

6

7

8

9

10 11 12 13

1868–70

1871-73

1 2 3

4 5 6

7 8 9 10

1874-75

1877–78

1 2 3 4 5 6 7 8 9 10 11 12

1888–90

1891-93

1894-95

1897–98

1901–1902

1903–1904

1905-1906

1907–1908

1 2 3 4 5 6 7 8 9 10 11 12 13 14 15

1909-10

1913–14

1 2 3 4 5 6 7 8 9 10 11 12 13 14 15 16 17 18 19

1917–18

1921–22

1923-24

1925—26

1929-30

NOTES ON THE SOURCES

FIRST CENTURY ♦ *Page 1:* 1. Roman lady of the Flavian period, 14–96, Vatican Museum. 2. Livia (d. 29), Museo Nazionale, Naples. 3. Titus (d. 81), Louvre, Paris. 4. Nerva (d. 98), Vatican Museum. 5. Poppaea (d. 65), Vatican Museum. 6. Minatia Polla, *c.*40, Museo delle Terme, Rome. 7. Marciana (d. 117), Pompeian Museum, Rome. 8. Augustus (d. 14), Altes Museum, Berlin. 9. Statue, *c.*1 A.D., Altes Museum, Berlin. 10. Statue, Museo Nazionale, Naples.

FIRST AND SECOND CENTURIES ♦ *Page 2:* 1. Drusus Caesar (d. 31), Museo Nazionale, Naples. 2. Livia (d. 29), Glyptothek, Copenhagen. 3. Augustus (d. 14), Capitol, Rome. 4. Statue, Vatican Museum. 5. Statue, just B.C., Vatican Museum. 6. The so-called Thusnelda, Loggia dei Lanzi, Florence. 7. Matidia, daughter of Trajan's sister (d. 117). 8. Roman lady, *c.*100, Museo Nazionale, Rome.

SECOND AND THIRD CENTURIES ♦ *Page 3:* 1. Commodus (d. 192), Vatican Museum. 2. Figure from Trajan's Column. 3. Faustina (d. 141), Vatican Museum. 4. Marcus Aurelius (d. 180), Statue in Venice. 5. Roman General from Trajan's Column. 6. Faustina the Younger (d. 175), Vatican Museum. 7. Marcus Aurelius (d. 180), Louvre, Paris. 8. Trajan (d. 119), Vatican Museum. 9. Lady, *c.*100, Capitoline Museum, Rome. 10. Matidia, daughter of Trajan's sister (d. 117). 11. Head of a woman, from Almendingen near Thun, *c.*300. 12. Statue of a Roman lady, 2nd cent., Palazzo Doria, Rome. 13. Statue of a Roman lady, 2nd cent., Glyptothek, Copenhagen.

FOURTH AND FIFTH CENTURIES ♦ *Page 4:* 1. Valentinian (d. 375), Statue in Barletta. 2. Julian the Apostate and his wife Helena, 361–3. 3. Ivory carving, 516. 4. Venice, *c.*400. 5. Stilicho, Regent of the Western Empire, with his wife Serena and son Eucharius, *c.*395.

SIXTH TO NINTH CENTURIES ♦ *Page 5:* 1–2. Santa Maria della Valle, Cividale, 7th–9th cent. 3. Figure from a Ravenna mosaic, 557–70. 4. Empress Theodora, 527–48. 5. Illumination, *c.*840, Fulda. 6. Justinian, mosaic in Ravenna, 546–48. 7. Empress Theodora and her Suite, mosaic in Ravenna, 546–48.

NINTH TO ELEVENTH CENTURIES ♦ *Page 6:* 1. Gospels of Otto III, end of the 10th cent. 2. Lectionary of the Salzburg School, Monastery of St Nikolaus, Passau, 2nd half of the 11th cent. 3. Psalterium aureum, St Gallen, 9th cent. 4–5. Miniatures, Paris, 11th cent. 6. Tombstone, St Emeran, Regensburg, 1001.

TWELFTH AND THIRTEENTH CENTURIES ♦ *Page 7:* 1. Notre Dame, Paris, 1165. 2. Minster in Westphalia, *c.*1100. 3. Illu-

mination, Halberstadt, *c.*1185. 4. Cathedral, Chartres, 13th century.

TWELFTH CENTURY ♦ *Page 8:* 1–4. Cathedral, Chartres. 5. Chapelle de Claviers, Cantal, *c.*1150. 6. Cologne, *c.*1150. 7. Cathedral, Chartres.

THIRTEENTH CENTURY ♦ *Page 9:* 1. Hermann. 2. Thietmar. 3. Reglindis. 4. Hermann. 5. Sizzo. 6. Reglindis (Statues in Naumburg Cathedral). ♦ *Page 10:* 1. Uta. 2. Wilhelm (Both statues in Naumburg Cathedral). 3. Synagogue, Strasbourg Cathedral, 1235–50. 4. Timo von Kistritz. 5. Ekkehard. 6. Uta. 7. Wil Wilhelm von Camberg. (4–7. Statues in Naumburg Cathedral) ♦ *Page 11:* 1. Emperor Otto I. 2–3. Gepa. 4. Empress Adelheid (Statues in Meissen Cathedral). 5. Cathedral, Rheims, 1250–70. 6. Empress Adelheid, Meissen Cathedral. ♦ *Page 12:* 1. Lady Gerburg. 2. Ekkehard. 3. Lady Gerburg (Statues in Naumburg Cathedral). 4. Cathedral Treasure, Minden, *c.*1300. 5. Dietrich, Naumburg Cathedral. ♦ *Page 13:* 1. Cathedral, Amiens. 2. Cathedral, Lincoln, before 1300. 3. Cathedral, Chartres, 1225–35. 4. Cathedral, Rheims, 1260–80 5–6. Cathedral, Chartres.

FOURTEENTH CENTURY ♦ *Page 14:* Manesse Codex, beginning of the century. ♦ *Page 15:* 1. Manesse Codex, beginning of the century. 2. Master of the Schönen Brunnen, Nuremberg, *c.*1400. 3, 5. Tombstone of Ulrich and Elizabeth von Erbach, 1368–69, Castle Erbach. 4. Anna von Schweidnitz, Prague Cathedral. ♦ *Page 16:* 1. Tombstone of Cinna von Vargula, 1370, Erfurt, Barfüsserkirche. 2. Adolph IV, Count von Holstein, painting in the Magdalenenstift, Hamburg, last quarter of the century. 3. Würzburg, *c.*1360. 4, 7. Tombstones of the Count von Hirschborn and his wife, 1370–71, Ersheim near Hirschborn. 5–6. Tombstone, Frankfurt Cathedral, 1371.

FIFTEENTH CENTURY ♦ *Page 17:* 1. French illumination, 1447. 2. Florentine, painted panel from a cassone, *c.*1440. 3. French illumination, 1447. 4. Andrea del Castagno, *c.*1420. 5. French illumination, 1447. 6. Andrea del Castagno, *c.*1450. 7. Attributed to Domenico Veneziano, *c.*1450. ♦ *Page 18:* 1. Master of the Housebook. 2. Rogier van der Weyden, *c.*1450. 3. Israel van Meckenem, before 1500. 4. Master of Moulins, 1494. 5. Albrecht Dürer, *Hans Tucher*, 1499. 6. Dürer, *c.*1500. 7, 8. I. van Meckenem, before 1500. 9. Dürer, *Elisabeth Tucher*, 1499. ♦ *Page 19:* 1–4. Antonio Pisanello, 1430–45. 5. Petrus Christus, 1446. 6–7. Antonio Pisanello, 1430–45. ♦ *Page 20:* 1. Rogier van der Weyden, 1435. 2. Jan van Eyck, 1434. 3–7. Jan van Eyck, second quarter of the century. ♦ *Page 21:* 1. French sculpture, beginning of the cent. 2. Anon. French Master, *c.*1440. 3. Jacopo della Quercia, tombstone in

Lucca Cathedral (?). 4. Masaccio, 1423. 5. Anon. French Master, *Jean sans Peur, Duke of Burgundy* (d. 1419). ♦ *Page 22:* 1. Albrecht Dürer, *Self-portrait,* 1484. 2. Domenico Ghirlandaio (d. 1494). 3. Lorenzo di Viterbo (d. 1469). 4. Anon. Florentine Master, mid cent. 5. L. di Viterbo (d. 1469). 6. Anon. French Master, *c.*1500. 7. L. di Viterbo (d. 1469). 8. Anon. Italian Master, *c.*1500. ♦ *Page 23:* 1. Dürer, *Self-portrait,* 1498. 2–3. Dürer, *c.*1500. 4–5. Dürer, 1495. 6. Dürer, *c.*1500. 7. North German Master, *c.*1500. 8. L. di Viterbo (d. 1469).

SIXTEENTH CENTURY ♦ *Page 24:* 1. Vittore Carpaccio, *c.*1500. 2. Hans Holbein the Younger, *c.*1520. 3. Dürer, 1515. 4. Holbein, *c.*1525. 5. Master of the Death of Mary, 1526. 6. Dürer, 1514. ♦ *Page 25:* 1. Urs Graf, beginning of the cent. 2. Holbein the Younger, *Sir George Cromwell, c.*1540. 3. Lucas Cranach the Elder, 1514. 4. Holbein, 1520. ♦ *Page 26:* 1. Dürer, 1515. 2. Holbein the Younger, *Self-portrait,* 1523–24. 3–5. Holbein, *c.*1520. ♦ *Page 27:* 1. Lucas van Leyden, 1519. 2. Lucas Cranach the Elder, 1524. 3. Michael Ostendorffer, 1545. 4. Holbein the Younger, *c.*1520. ♦ *Page 28:* 1. School of Holbein the Younger, *Edward VI, c.*1550. 2. Plumed cap and its original box, once owned by Christoph Kress von Kressenstein, German Museum, Nuremberg. 3. Holbein the Younger, *c.*1520. 4. Urs Graf, beginning of the cent. 5. Angelo Bronzino, *c.*1545. 6. Holbein, *c.*1520. ♦ *Page 29:* 1. Bronzino, 1553–55. 2. François Clouet (d. 1571), *Charles IX of France as a boy.* 3. Jost Amman, 1577. 4. Antonio Moro, *c.*1560. ♦ *Page 30:* 1. François Clouet, *Maria Stuart,* 1558. 2–3. Jost Amman, *c.*1570. 4. *Queen Elizabeth, wife of Charles IX, c.*1570. 5. J. Amman, *c.*1570. 6. Holbein the Younger, 1551. 7. J. Amman, *c.*1570. 8. F. Clouet, *Charles IX of France,* 1560–74. ♦ *Page 31:* 1. German woodcut, end of the cent. 2. Moro, 1564. 3–4. German woodcuts, end of the cent. 5. Bronzino, mid cent. 6. Lucas Cranach the Younger, 1564. 7. Cano, *c.*1560. 8. Holbein the Younger, 1551. ♦ *Page 32:* 1. Cranach the Younger, 1564. 2. Tobias Stimmer, 1564. 3. French School, *c.*1558. 4. Cranach the Younger, 1564. 5. Pietro Bertelli, *Femina Parisiana,* 1590. 6. French School, 1575–80. 7. Jost Amman, 1577. 8. French School, *c.*1550. 9. Bronzino, *c.*1560. ♦ *Page 33:* 1. Jost Amman, 1577. 2. Adam vom Oirt, *c.*1590. 3. French School, *c.*1560. 4–6. Italian engravings of French fashions, *c.*1580. 7. Dutch Master, *c.*1580. ♦ *Page 34:* 1–3. Cesare Vecellio (Spain), 1590. 4–5. Eneas Vico (Spain), 1556. 6. Jacob de Gheyn, *c.*1590. 7. Italian engraving of French fashion. 8. Vico (Spain), 1556. 9. Vecellio (Spain), *c.*1590. 10. Vico (Spain), 1556.

SEVENTEENTH CENTURY ♦ *Page 35:* 1–9. de St Igny, 1629. 10–13. F. Bruns, 1617. ♦ *Page 36:* 1. de St Igny, *c.*1630. 2. Rubens, *Susanne Fourment,* 1620. 3–4. de St Igny, *c.*1630. 5. German Museum, Nuremberg, *c.*1620. 6. de St Igny, *c.*1630. 7–11. Willem Buytewech, 1617. ♦ *Page 37:* 1. de St Igny, 1629. 2. Abraham Bosse, *c.*1630. 3. Van Dyck, *Jacques Callot, c.*1630. 4. de St Igny, *c.*1630. 5. Callot, *c.*1630. 6–7. Israel Henriet, *c.*1630. 8–9. Callot, 1632. 10–11. Callot, *c.*1630. ♦ *Page 38:* 1. Abraham Bosse, 1633. 2. Le Blond, *c.*1630. 3. Stefano della Bella, *c.*1630. 4. Grégoire Huret, *c.*1630. 5. Bosse, 1629. ♦ *Page 39:* 1. Gerard Terborch, 1645. 2–3. Wenceslaus Hollar (England), 1641. 4. Hollar, 1643. 5. Terborch, 1640. 6. Terborch, 1656. 7. Terborch, *c.*1640.

8–9. Van Dyck, 1641. ♦ *Page 40:* 1. Van Dyck, *Sir Arthur Goodwin,* 1639. 2. Terborch, *c.*1660. 3. Van Dyck, *Sir Thomas Wharton,* 1639. 4–8. Hollar (England), 1643–4. ♦ *Page 41:* 1–2. Hollar (England), 1647. 3. Bartholomaeus van der Helst, 1642. 4. Hollar (England), 1647. 5. Terborch, 1663–4. 6. B. van der Helst, 1649. 7. Caspar Netscher, 1665. 8. Terborch, *c.*1650. 9. Antoine le Nain, 1647. 10. Velazquez, *The Infant Prince Balthasar Carlos,* 1635–6. 11. Terborch, *c.*1640. ♦ *Page 42:* 1. de St Jean, 1678. 2. de St Jean, 1683. 3. French engraving, end of the cent. 4–5. de St Jean, 1678–84. 6. Hyacinthe Rigaud, *Duchesse de Mentone.* 7. Carguillière, end of the cent. 8. Carolus Allard, 1680. ♦ *Page 43:* 1. Hyacinthe Rigaud, end of the cent. 2. de St Jean, 1684. 3. Rigaud, end of the cent. 4. Anon. engraving, end of the cent. 5–7. de St Jean, 1684. 8. Victoria and Albert Museum, end of the cent. ♦ *Page 44:* 1. Italian fashion plate, 1689. 2. G. Valck, end of the cent. 3. de St Jean, 1683. 4. G. Valck, end of the cent. 5. de St Jean, *c.*1680. 6. G. Valck, end of the cent.

1700–10 ♦ *Page 45:* 1. Peter Schenk, *Wife of Augustus the Strong, c.*1700. 2. Hyacinthe Rigaud, *c.*1700. 3. M. Wolffgang, *c.*1700. 4–5. Jacobus Gole, *c.*1700. 6. Nicolas Guérard, *c.*1700.

1711–20 ♦ *Page 46:* 1. Antoine Watteau, 1719–21. 2. Watteau, 1716–18. 3. Watteau, 1719. 4. Anon. French Master, *c.*1720. 5. Watteau, 1716–18. ♦ *Page 47:* 1. Watteau, 1719–21. 2. Watteau, 1716–18. 3. François Boucher, *c.*1720. 4–5. Watteau, 1719–21.

1721–30 ♦ *Page 48:* 1. Jean de Troy, 1725. 2. Jean Baptiste Chardin, *c.*1730. 3. Nicolas Lancret, *c.*1725. 4. Nicolas de Largillière, *c.*1730. 5. Lancret, *c.*1725.

1731–40 ♦ *Page 49:* 1. Cornelius Trost, 1737. 2–3. Jean de Troy, 1731. 4. André Portail. 5. Nicolas Lancret, 1735. 6. William Hogarth, 1740.

1741–50 ♦ *Page 50:* 1. Canot, 1745. 2. Aubert, 1747. 3. Canot, 1745. 4–6. Canot, 1747. 7. Noël Coypel, *Mme Pompadour,* 1746. 8. Boucher, *c.*1750. ♦ *Page 51:* 1. Pietro Longhi, *c.*1750. 2. Etienne Liotard, 1746–47. 3. Jean-Marc Nattier, *c.*1740. 4. William Hogarth, 1745. 5. Boucher, *Mme Pompadour,* 1750. 6. Longhi, *c.*1740.

1751–60 ♦ *Page 52:* 1. François Boucher, *Mme Pompadour,* 1752. 2. Sir Joshua Reynolds, 1760. 3–4. Boucher, *Mme Pompadour,* 1750. 5. Honoré Fragonard, *c.*1760. ♦ *Page 53:* 1. Glume, *c.*1750. 2. P. A. Wille, 1760. 3. Justus Chevillet, 1760. 4. Maurice Quentin de la Tour, *Mme Pompadour.* 5. Thomas Gainsborough, 1760.

1761–70 ♦ *Page 54:* 1. J. B. Huet, *c.*1765. 2. Anon. miniature, 1765. 3–4. Jean Baptiste Greuze, *c.*1770. 5. Battoni, 1768. 6. T. Gainsborough, 1765. ♦ *Page 55:* 1. de St Aubin, *c.*1770. 2. T. Gainsborough, 1765. 3. de St Aubin, *c.*1770. 4. H. Fragonard, *c.*1770. 5. J. B. Huet, 1770.

1771–80 ♦ *Page 56:* 1–8. Peter Schenk, 1775. ♦ *Page 57:* 1–4. Galerie des Modes, 1776. 5. Galerie des Modes, 1778. 6. T. Gainsborough, *c.*1775. 7. Jean Duclos, 1778. 8. Galerie des Modes, 1779.

1781–90 ♦ *Page 58:* 1. Journal des Luxus und der Moden, 1784. 2. Journal des Modes, 1786. 3. Journal des Luxus und der Moden, 1787. 4. Journal des Modes, 1786. 5. Journal des Luxus und der Moden, 1788. 6. Journal des Luxus und der Moden, 1790. 7. Reynolds, 1789. ♦ *Page 59:* 1. Elizabeth-Louise Vigée-Lebrun, *Marie Antoinette,* 1783. 2. Reynolds, 1786. 3. Hoppner, *c.*1785. 4. William Ward, 1788. 5. Roslin, 1782. 6. G. K. Urlaub, 1785. ♦ *Page 60:* 1. Downman, *c.*1785. 2–3. Mme Vigée-Lebrun, 1790. 4. Lawrence, 1790. 5. Mme Vigée-Lebrun, *c.*1790.

1791–92 ♦ *Page 61:* 1–6. Journal des Luxus und der Moden, 1791. 7–14. Journal des Luxus und der Moden, 1792.

1793–94 ♦ *Page 62:* 1–6. Journal des Luxus und der Moden, 1793. 7. Gallery of Fashion, 1794. 8. Journal des Luxus und der Moden, 1794. 9–10. Gallery of Fashion, 1794.

1795–96 ♦ *Page 63:* 1. Allgemeines Europäisches Journal, 1796. 2. Gallery of Fashion, 1796. 3–4. Allgemeines Europäisches Journal, 1796. 5. Journal des Luxus und der Moden, 1795. 6. Gallery of Fashion, 1796. 7. François Gérard, 1795. ♦ *Page 64:* 1. Journal des Luxus und der Moden, 1795. 2–3. François Gérard, 1796. 4–5. Journal des Luxus und der Moden, 1796. 6. Gallery of Fashion, 1796. 7. Jacques Louis David, *Self-portrait,* 1795. 8. J. L. David, 1795. 9. Journal des Luxus und der Moden, 1795. 10. Allgemeines Europäisches Journal, 1795.

1797–98 ♦ *Page 65:* 1. Journal des Luxus und der Moden, 1797. 2–3. Gallery of Fashion, 1798. 4. Gallery of Fashion, 1797. 5–6. Journal des Luxus und der Moden, 1797. 7–8. Gallery of Fashion, 1797. 9. Journal des Luxus und der Moden, 1798. 10–11. Gallery of Fashion, 1798.

1799–1800 ♦ *Page 66:* 1. Journal des Luxus und der Moden, 1800. 2–3. Gallery of Fashion, 1799. 4–5. Journal des Luxus und der Moden, 1799. 6. Gallery of Fashion, 1799. 7. Journal des Luxus und der Moden, 1800. 8. François Gérard, *Mme de Staël, c.*1800. 9–10. Gallery of Fashion, 1800.

1800–3 ♦ *Page 67:* 1. Charis, 1801. 2. Journal des Modes, 1902. 3. Journal des Luxus und der Moden, 1801. 4. Journal des Luxus und der Moden, 1803. 5. Journal des Modes, 1803. 6. Johann Heinrich Schröder, *Queen Luise of Prussia, c.*1800. 7. Charis, 1803. 8. Journal des Luxus und der Moden, 1800. 9. Journal des Luxus und der Moden, 1801. 10. Journal des Luxus und der Moden, 1802. 11. Journal des Modes, 1802. 12. Journal des Modes, 1800.

1804–7 ♦ *Page 68:* 1–2. Costume Parisien, 1804. 3. Jean Auguste Dominique Ingres, *Philibert Rivière.* 4–5. Costume Parisien, 1805. 6–11. Journal des Dames, 1806. 12. Costume Parisien, 1804. 13. Costume Parisien, 1805. 14. Ingres, *Mme Récamier.* 15. Costume Parisien, 1807. 16. Journal des Dames, 1807.

1808–10 ♦ *Page 69:* 1–2. Journal des Dames, 1810. 3. Zeitung für die elegante Welt, 1810. 4. Journal des Dames, 1810. 5. Zeitung für die elegante Welt, 1810. 6–8. Records of Fashion, 1808. 9–11. Costume Parisien, 1808. 12. Allgemeine Modenzeitung, 1809. 13. Records of Fashion, 1809.

1811–13 ♦ *Page 70:* 1–2. Journal des Dames, 1813. 3–4. Allgemeine Modenzeitung, 1813. 5–10. Journal des Dames, 1812. 11. Allgemeine Modenzeitung, 1811. 12–14. Journal des Dames, 1811. 15. Allgemeine Modenzeitung, 1811. 16. Journal des Dames, 1811.

1814–17 ♦ *Page 71:* 1–2. Allgemeine Modenzeitung, 1814. 3. Journal des Dames, 1815, 1817. 4–5. Journal des Dames, 1815. 6–7. Journal des Dames, 1816. 8. Ingres, *Mme Ingres.* 9. Journal des Dames, 1816. 10. Journal des Dames, 1815. 11–16. Journal des Dames, 1817.

1818–21 ♦ *Page 72:* 1. Journal des Dames, 1818. 2. The Lady's Magazine, 1818. 3. Journal des Dames, 1818. 4. The Lady's Magazine, 1818. 5–7. Journal des Luxus und der Moden, 1819. 8–9. Journal des Luxus und der Moden, 1820. 10–12. The Lady's Magazine, 1820. 13–14. Journal des Dames, 1821. 15–16. Fashion Plates, 1821. 17. The Lady's Magazine, 1821.

1822–24 ♦ *Page 73:* 1. Allgemeine Modenzeitung, 1822. 2. Observateur de la Mode, 1822. 3–5. Allgemeine Modenzeitung, 1822. 6–8. Allgemeine Modenzeitung, 1823. 9. Rossini, *Lithograph,* 1823. 10–11. Observateur de la Mode, 1823. 11–15. Allgemeine Modenzeitung, 1824.

1825–27 ♦ *Page 74:* 1. Journal des Dames et des Modes, 1825. 2. Journal des Dames et des Modes, 1827. 3–4. Journal des Dames, 1825. 5. Journal des Dames et des Modes, 1827. 6. Journal des Dames, 1825. 7. Journal des Dames et des Modes, 1827. 8. Journal des Dames et des Modes, 1825 9. Journal des Dames, 1827. 10–11. *The Singer Constance Tibaldi and Dr Goll* (after an engraving), 1825. 12–13. Journal des Dames et des Modes, 1827. 14. Journal des Luxus und der Moden, 1826. 15–17. Journal des Dames, 1826. 18. Journal des Dames et des Modes, 1826. 19. Journal des Dames et des Modes, 1827.

1828–30 ♦ *Page 75:* 1. Allgemeine Modenzeitung, 1828. 2. Allgemeine Modenzeitung, 1830. 3. After a lithograph dated 1830. 4. Allgemeine Modenzeitung, 1831. 5–6. Allgemeine Modenzeitung, 1829. 7. Journal des Dames et des Modes, 1829. 8. Journal des Dames et des Modes, 1830. 9–10. Journal des Dames et des Modes, 1828. 11–14. Allgemeine Modenzeitung, 1830. 15. Journal des Dames et des Modes, 1830. 16. Allgemeine Modenzeitung, 1828.

1831–32 ♦ *Page 76:* 1–2. Allgemeine Modenzeitung, 1831. 3–5. Journal des Dames et des Modes, 1831. 6. Allgemeine Modenzeitung, 1832. 7. *Queen Amélie of France* from a lithograph, 1831. 8. Journal des Dames et des Modes, 1831. 9–13. Journal des Dames et des Modes, 1832.

1833–1835 ♦ *Page 77:* 1–3. Allgemeine Modenzeitung, 1834. 4. Les Modes Parisiennes, 1834. 5. Allgemeine Modenzeitung, 1834. 6. Allgemeine Modenzeitung, 1835. 7. Allgemeine Modenzeitung, 1833. 8–9. *Judith and Julie Grisil, singers in the Italian Opera in Paris,* from a lithograph, 1834. 10. Allgemeine Modenzeitung, 1834. 11–12. Allgemeine Modenzeitung, 1833. 13. Le Voleur, 1834. 14. Modes de Paris, 1834.

1835–37 ♦ *Page 78:* 1–3. Allgemeine Modenzeitung, 1835. 4–5. The Monthly Belle Assemblée, 1835. 6. *Isabel, Queen of Spain,* lithograph, 1835. 7. *Victoria, Queen of England,* lithograph, 1835. 8. *George Sand,* lithograph, 1837. 9. Journal des Dames, 1836. 10. Allgemeine Modenzeitung, 1836. 11. *Johann Strauss,* lithograph, 1836. 12. The Monthly Belle Assemblée, 1836. 13. Allgemeine Modenzeitung, 1836. 14. Allgemeine Modenzeitung, 1837. 15–16. The Monthly Belle Assemblée, 1837. 17. Allgemeine Modenzeitung, 1837.

1838–40 ♦ *Page 79:* 1–5. Allgemeine Modenzeitung, 1840. 6. Modes de Paris, 1839. 7. *Daguerre,* lithograph, 1839. 8. *The Singer Duprès,* lithograph, 1839. 9. Lithograph, 1838. 10. *Clara Wieck,* lithograph, 1839. 11–13. Modes de Paris, 1838. 14–16. Modes de Paris, 1839.

1841–44 ♦ *Page 80:* 1. *Alfred de Vigny,* 1841. 2. *The Singer Carlotta Grisi,* 1842. 3. *Princesse de Joinville,* 1842. 4. *Franz Liszt,* 1843. 5. *Albert Lortzing,* 1843. 6. Allgemeine Modenzeitung, 1842. 7. Journal des Dames, 1843. 8. Journal des Dames, 1842. 9. Allgemeine Modenzeitung, 1841. 10. Allgemeine Modenzeitung, 1842. 11. Le Moniteur de la Mode, 1844. 12. Allgemeine Modenzeitung, 1844. 13. Allgemeine Modenzeitung, 1842. 14. Pariser Modejournal, 1841. 15. Allgemeine Modenzeitung, 1841. 16–17. Journal des Dames, 1842. 18. Allgemeine Modenzeitung, 1842.

1845–47 ♦ *Page 81:* 1–4. Allgemeine Modenzeitung, 1845. 5. Le Moniteur de la Mode, 1845. 6. Allgemeine Modenzeitung, 1845. 7. *Verdi,* lithograph, 1847. 8. *Emanual Geibel,* lithograph, 1847. 9. Allgemeine Modenzeitung, 1847. 10–11. Journal des Dames, 1846. 12. Le Moniteur de la Mode, 1847. 13. Le Moniteur de la Mode, 1846. 14. Journal des Dames, 1847.

1848–50 ♦ *Page 82:* 1–3. Allgemeine Modenzeitung, 1850. 4–5. Allgemeine Modenzeitung, 1848. 6. Le Moniteur de la Mode, 1850. 7. Lithograph, 1849. 8. *Proudhon,* lithograph, 1850. 9. *Sir Henry Lytton Bulwer,* lithograph, 1850. 10. Le Moniteur de la Mode, 1850. 11. Allgemeine Modenzeitung, 1849. 12–14. Le Moniteur de la Mode, 1849. 15. Allgemeine Modenzeitung, 1848.

1851–52 ♦ *Page 83:* 1. Lithograph, 1852. 2–3. Allgemeine Modenzeitung, 1851. 4. Le Moniteur de la Mode, 1852. 5. *Ludwig Richter,* lithograph, 1852. 6. Allgemeine Modenzeitung, 1851. 7. Wiener Elegante, 1851. 8. *The Singer Johanna Wagner,* lithograph, 1852. 9–10. Allgemeine Modenzeitung, 1851. 11. Wiener Elegante, 1852. 12–13. Europäische Modenzeitung, 1852. 14. Allgemeine Modenzeitung, 1851. 15. Allgemeine Modenzeitung, 1852.

1853–54 ♦ *Page 84:* 1. Le Moniteur de la Mode, 1854. 2. Wiener Elegante, 1854. 3. Allgemeine Modenzeitung, 1854. 4–6. Le Moniteur de la Mode, 1853. 7–8. Allgemeine Modenzeitung, 1854. 9–11. Le Moniteur de la Mode, 1854. 12–13. Allgemeine Modenzeitung, 1854. 14. Allgemeine Modenzeitung, 1853. 15. Europäische Modenzeitung, 1853. 16–19. Allgemeine Modenzeitung, 1853.

1855–57 ♦ *Page 85:* 1–4. Allgemeine Modenzeitung, 1857. 5. Europäische Modenzeitung, 1855. 6. Allgemeine Modenzeitung, 1855. 7–8. Der Bazar, 1855. 9. Europäische Modenzeitung, 1856. 10. L'Observateur de Modes, 1857. 11. Penelope, 1855. 12. Der Bazar, 1855. 13. L'Observateur des Modes, 1856.

1858–60 ♦ *Page 86:* 1. Europäische Modenzeitung, 1858. 2–3. L'Iris, 1858. 4. Europäische Modenzeitung, 1859. 5. L'Iris, 1859. 6–7. Les Modes Parisiennes, 1860. 8. L'Iris, 1859. 9. Europäische Modenzeitung, 1860. 10–11. Allgemeine Modenzeitung, 1860. 12. Europäische Modenzeitung, 1860.

1861–62 ♦ *Page 87:* 1. Der Bazar, 1862. 2. Le Moniteur de la Mode, 1862. 3–4. Der Bazar, 1862. 5. Allgemeine Modenzeitung, 1862. 6. Allgemeine Modenzeitung, 1862. 7. Le Moniteur de la Mode, 1861. 8–10. Allgemeine Modenzeitung, 1862. 11. Europäische Modenzeitung, 1862. 12. Le Moniteur de la Mode, 1862. 13. Le Moniteur de la Mode, 1861. 14. Der Bazar, 1861. 15. Le Moniteur de la Mode, 1861. 16–17. Allgemeine Modenzeitung, 1861.

1863–64 ♦ *Page 88:* 1. Europäische Modenzeitung, 1864. 2–3. Courier des Dames, 1864. 4–6. Allgemeine Modenzeitung, 1864. 7. Der Bazar, 1863. 8. Der Bazar, 1864. 9–10. Der Bazar, 1863. 11. Les Modes Parisiennes, 1863. 12. Europäische Modenzeitung, 1863. 13. Europäische Modenzeitung, 1864.

1865–67 ♦ *Page 89:* 1. Allgemeine Modenzeitung, 1865 2. Le Moniteur de la Mode, 1865. 3–5. Allgemeine Modenzeitung, 1866. 6–7. Le Moniteur de la Mode, 1865. 8. Allgemeine Modenzeitung, 1865. 9–10. Allgemeine Modenzeitung, 1866. 11. Le Moniteur de la Mode, 1867. 12–13. Allgemeine Modenzeitung, 1867. 14. Europäische Modenzeitung, 1865. 15. Allgemeine Modenzeitung, 1867. 16. Europäische Modenzeitung, 1867.

1868–70 ♦ *Page 90:* 1–2. Der Bazar, 1868. 3. *Victoria,* 1868. 4. Allgemeine Modenzeitung, 1868. 5. Der Bazar, 1868. 6. Le Moniteur de la Mode, 1870. 7. Der Bazar, 1870. 8. Le Moniteur de la Mode, 1869. 9. Le Moniteur de la Mode, 1870. 10–11. Der Bazar, 1869. 12. Europäische Modenzeitung, 1868. 13. Der Bazar, 1869. ♦ *Page 91:* 1–2. Der Bazar, 1870. 3. Le Moniteur de la Mode, 1868. 4. L'Art et la Mode, 1869. 5. Europäische Modenzeitung, 1868. 6. Le Moniteur de la Mode, 1869. 7–8. Der Bazar, 1868. 9. Der Bazar, 1870. 10. Europäische Modenzeitung, 1868. 11. Le Moniteur de la Mode, 1870. 12. Der Bazar, 1868. 13. Der Bazar, 1870.

1871–73 ♦ *Page 92:* 1. Europäische Modenzeitung, 1873. 2. Allgemeine Modenzeitung, 1873. 3. Le Moniteur de la Mode, 1873. 4. Allgemeine Modenzeitung, 1873. 5. Europäische Modenzeitung, 1872. 6–7. Der Bazar, 1871. 8. Der Bazar, 1871. 9. Der Bazar, 1873. 10. Der Bazar, 1872. 11. Le Moniteur de la Mode, 1871. 12. Le Moniteur de la Mode, 1873. 13–14. Allgemeine Modenzeitung, 1873. 15. Der Bazar, 1872. 16–17. Allgemeine Modenzeitung, 1873.

1874–75 ♦ *Page 93:* 1. Der Bazar, 1874. 2. Le Moniteur de la Mode, 1875. 3. Le Moniteur de la Mode, 1874. 4. Der Bazar, 1874. 5. Der Bazar, 1875. 6. Le Moniteur de la Mode, 1874. 7. Europäische Modenzeitung, 1874. 8–9. Der Bazar, 1875. 10. Europäische Modenzeitung, 1875.

1876 ♦ *Page 94:* 1–2. Europäische Modenzeitung, 1876. 3. Der Bazar, 1876. 4–5. Les Modes Parisiennes, 1876. 6. Le Moniteur de la Mode, 1876. 7. Der Bazar, 1876. 8. Allgemeine Modenzeitung, 1876. 9. Allgemeine Modenzeitung, 1876. 10–12. Der Bazar, 1876.

1877–78 ♦ *Page 95:* 1–2. Der Bazar, 1877. 3. Europäische Modenzeitung, 1877. 4–8. Der Bazar, 1877. 9–10. Der Bazar, 1878. 11. Der Bazar, 1877. 12. Allgemeine Modenzeitung, 1878. 13–14. Le Moniteur de la Mode, 1878. 15–17. Allgemeine Modenzeitung, 1878. 18. Der Bazar, 1877.

1878–80 ♦ *Page 96:* 1–2. Der Bazar, 1879. 3. Der Bazar, 1880. 4. Europäische Modenzeitung, 1880. 5–6. Der Bazar, 1878. 7. Der Bazar, 1879. 8. Europäische Modenzeitung, 1880. 9. Der Bazar, 1879. 10. Der Bazar, 1880. 11–13. Europäische Modenzeitung, 1880. 14. Der Bazar, 1880.

1881–83 ♦ *Page 97:* 1. Journal des Dames et des Modes, 1883. 2. Europäische Modenzeitung, 1882. 3. Le Moniteur de la Mode, 1881. 4. Europäische Modenzeitung, 1883. 5. Illustrierte Frauenzeitung, 1881. 6. Journal des Dames et des Modes, 1883. 7. Europäische Modenzeitung, 1882. 8–9. Le Moniteur de la Mode, 1882. 10. Journal des Dames et des Modes, 1882. 11. Le Moniteur de la Mode, 1881. 12. Journal des Dames et des Modes, 1881.

1884–85 ♦ *Page 98:* 1–2. Europäische Modenzeitung, 1884. 3. Le Moniteur de la Mode, 1885. 4. Europäische Modenzeitung, 1884. 5. Le Moniteur de la Mode, 1884. 6. Europäische Modenzeitung, 1885. 7. Der Bazar, 1884. 8. Le Moniteur de la Mode, 1884. 9. Allgemeine Modenzeitung, 1885. 10. Europäische Modenzeitung, 1885. 11–12. Le Moniteur de la Mode, 1884.

1886–87 ♦ *Page 99:* 1–4. Europäische Modenzeitung, 1887. 5–6. Le Moniteur de la Mode, 1887. 7–8. Der Bazar, 1887. 9. Europäische Modenzeitung, 1887. 10. Allgemeine Modenzeitung, 1886. 11–13. Der Bazar, 1886. 14. Allgemeine Modenzeitung, 1886. 15. Le Moniteur de la Mode, 1887. 16. Der Bazar, 1887.

1888–90 ♦ *Page 100:* 1. Europäische Modenzeitung, 1889. 2. La Modiste Universelle, 1890. 3–4. Der Bazar, 1889. 5. Le Moniteur de la Mode, 1890. 6–7. Der Bazar, 1888. 8. Le Moniteur de la Mode, 1889. 9. Der Bazar, 1890.

1891–93 ♦ *Page 101:* 1. Europäische Modenzeitung, 1893. 2–3. Allgemeine Modenzeitung, 1893. 4. Le Moniteur de la Mode, 1892. 5. Europäische Modenzeitung, 1893. 6–7. Le Moniteur de la Mode, 1891. 8. Der Bazar, 1893. 9. Le Moniteur de la Mode, 1892. 10. Wiener Mode, 1892. 11. Wiener Modenzeitung, 1892.

1894–95 ♦ *Page 102:* 1. Der Beobachter, 1894. 2. Der Bazar, 1895. 3. Wiener Mode, 1895. 4. Le Moniteur de la Mode, 1895. 5. Der Bazar, 1895. 6–7. Der Bazar, 1894. 8–9. Le Moniteur de la Mode, 1894. 10. Wiener Mode, 1894. 11. Le Moniteur de la Mode, 1895.

1896 ♦ *Page 103:* 1. Der Bazar, 1896. 2. Wiener Mode, 1896. 3. Le Moniteur de la Mode, 1896. 4. Der Bazar, 1896. 5. Le Moniteur de la Mode, 1896. 6. The Sartorial Art Journal, 1896. 7. Der Bazar, 1896. 8. Le Moniteur de la Mode, 1896. 9. Der Bazar, 1896.

1897–98 ♦ *Page 104:* 1. Le Moniteur de la Mode, 1898. 2–4. Le Salon de la Mode, 1897. 5. Le Moniteur de la Mode, 1898. 6. Wiener Mode, 1898. 7. Le Moniteur de la Mode, 1898. 8. Le Salon de la Mode, 1897. 9. Europäische Modenzeitung, 1898.

1899–1900 ♦ *Page 105:* 1. Wiener Mode, 1900. 2. Le Salon de la Mode, 1900. 3. Le Salon de la Mode, 1899. 4. Le Moniteur de la Mode, 1900. 5. Le Salon de la Mode, 1899. 6. Europäische Modenzeitung, 1899. 7. Wiener Mode, 1900. 8. Myra's Journal, London, 1899.

1901–2 ♦ *Page 106:* 1–2. Wiener Mode, 1902. 3. Les Modes, 1902. 4. Wiener Mode, 1901. 5–6. Wiener Mode, 1902. 7. Les Modes, 1901. 8. The Tailor Review, 1902. 9–10. Wiener Mode, 1902.

1903–4 ♦ *Page 107:* 1. Wiener Mode, 1903. 2–4. Illustrierte Frauenzeitung, 1903. 5–8. Wiener Mode, 1904. 9. Wiener Mode, 1903. 10. Die Modenwelt, 1904. 11. Wiener Mode, 1904. 12. Europäische Modenzeitung, 1903. 13. Wiener Mode, 1904.

1905–6 ♦ *Page 108:* 1–2. Wiener Mode, 1906. 3. Wiener Mode, 1905. 4. Les Modes, 1905. 5. Wiener Mode, 1906. 6. Illustrierte Frauenzeitung, 1906. 7. Wiener Mode, 1905. 8–9. Les Modes, 1905. 10. Illustrierte Frauenzeitung, 1906.

1907–8 ♦ *Page 109:* 1–2. Wiener Mode, 1907. 3–4. Les Modes, 1907. 5. Wiener Mode, 1908. 6–7. Illustrierte Frauenzeitung, 1908. 8. *The Actress Réjane,* Photo, 1908. 9. Les Modes, 1908. 10. Les Modes, 1907. 11. Illustrierte Frauenzeitung, 1908. 12. Wiener Mode, 1908.

1909–10 ♦ *Page 110:* 1–2. Illustrierte Frauenzeitung, 1910. 3–5. Wiener Mode, 1910. 6–7. Illustrierte Frauenzeitung, 1910. 8. Wiener Mode, 1909. 9. Deutsche Allgemeine Frauenzeitung, 1909. 10. Illustrierte Frauenzeitung, 1909. 11–12. Les Modes, 1909. 13–15. Wiener Mode, 1910.

1911–12 ♦ *Page 111:* 1. Illustrierte Frauenzeitung, 1911. 2. Wiener Mode, 1912. 3. Les Modes, 1912. 4. Wiener Mode, 1912. 5. Illustrierte Frauenzeitung, 1911. 6. Die Dame, 1912. 7. Les Modes, 1912. 8–11. Die Dame, 1912. 12. Wiener Mode, 1911. 13–15. Die Dame, 1912.

1913–14 ♦ *Page 112:* 1. Wiener Mode, 1913. 2. Offizielle Friseurzeitung, 1914. 3–4. Die Dame, 1914. 5–6. Wiener

Mode, 1913. 7. Die Dame, 1913. 8. Les Modes, 1913. 9. Die Dame, 1913. 10. Les Modes, 1914. 11–14. Die Dame, 1914.

1915–16 ◆ *Page 113:* 1. Die Herrenwelt, 1916. 2. Vogue, 1916. 3–4. Allgemeine Friseurzeitung, 1916. 5–6. Die Herrenkleidung, 1916. 7. Die Dame, 1916. 8. Die Herrenkleidung, 1916. 9. Die Herrenwelt, 1915. 10. Die Dame, 1915. 11. Die Dame, 1916. 12. Die Herrenkleidung, 1916. 13. Vogue, 1916. 14–15. Die Dame, 1916. 16–17. Vogue, 1916. 18–19. Die Dame, 1915.

1917–18 ◆ *Page 114:* 1. Der Herr, 1917. 2. Vogue, 1918. 3. Wiener Mode, 1917. 4. Die Dame, 1918. 5. Europäische Modenzeitung, 1918. 6. Vogue, 1918. 7. Allgemeine Friseurzeitung, 1917. 8–10. Die Dame, 1917. 11–13. Wiener Modenzeitung, 1918. 14. Wiener Mode, 1917. 15. Der Herr, 1917. 16. Die Dame, 1917.

1919–20 ◆ *Page 115:* 1. Femina, 1920. 2. Vogue, 1920. 3. Die Dame (*Fritzi Massary*), 1919. 4. Vogue, 1919. 5. Photo Binder, 1920. 6–8. Die Dame, 1920. 9. Der Herr, 1920. 10–11. Femina, 1919. 12. Der Herr, 1919.

1921–22 ◆ *Page 116:* 1. Vogue, 1922. 2. Femina, 1922. 3–4. Femina, 1921. 5. Die Dame, 1921. 6–8. Die Dame, 1922. 9. Die Dame, 1921. 10–15. Die Dame, 1922. 16. Die Dame, 1921. 17. Der Herr, 1921.

1923–24 ◆ *Page 117:* 1–2. Die Dame, 1923. 3. Internationale Moden, 1923. 4. Die Dame, 1923. 5. Internationale Moden, 1923. 6. Die Dame, 1923. 7–15. Chiffon, 1924.

1925–26 ◆ *Page 118:* 1–2. Die Dame, 1926. 3–5. Chiffon, 1925. 6–8. Offizielle Friseurzeitung, 1925. 9. Die Dame, 1925. 10–13. Chiffon, 1926. 14. Internationale Moden, 1926. 15–16. Chiffon, 1925.

1927–28 ◆ *Page 119:* 1–2. Der Modediktator, 1928. 3. Chiffon, 1927. 4. Die Dame, 1928. 5–6. Chiffon, 1927. 7. Chiffon, 1928. 8. Chiffon, 1927. 9. Femina, 1928. 10. Chiffon, 1927. 11. Der Modediktator, 1928.

1929–30 ◆ *Page 120:* 1. Femina, 1929. 2–5. Die Dame, 1930. 6. Femina, 1929. 7. Die Dame, 1930. 8. Chiffon, 1929. 9. Die Neue Linie, 1930. 10–11. Chiffon, 1929. 12. Die Neue Linie, 1930.